_____ Uncovering th

Bob Horrocks is married to Judie and they have two grown-up children. After twenty two years of ordained ministry within the Church of England he is now Team Rector of a large urban parish in the Diocese of Manchester. Evangelical by conversion and conviction he stumbled into Naturism in 2004 and had to re-evaluate his received theology and his reading of the Bible to see where God was leading him. He embarked on a journey of discovery and saw new emphases in the scriptures which he believes were previously hidden beneath layers of evangelical tradition and contemporary culture. He is presently Chair of the Christian Naturist Fellowship alongside his parish ministry. What follows is his personal understanding of his present position. His hope is that more people will be open to what is in the biblical tradition without the blinkers which prevent us from fully evaluating the text. Through that process he believes that more people will appreciate the freedom that comes through Jesus Christ and come to rediscover the image of God which lives in us.

Uncovering the Image

BOB HORROCKS

A revelation and a re-evaluation
of faith, the body and the bible

"So God created human beings in his own image,
in the image of God he created them;
male and female he created them."
Genesis 1:27

CONTENTS

Preface - 4

Chapter

1   A new beginning - 6

2   Where to now? - 11

3   A sign of the Covenant - 22

4   What did Jesus do? - 27

5   Concrete objections? - 30

6   But is it art? - 39

7   Brave Nude World - 42

8   Naked by Nature - 50

Appendix 1 – British Naturism Briefing Paper "Naturist Beliefs" - 56

Appendix 2 - British Naturism Briefing Paper "Statistics" - 58

Bibliography - 64

PREFACE

To mention the words Christian and Naturist in the same sentence or even to believe that the two can co-exist within an individual may seem anathema to some. At one time in my life that would have been the case for me. How is it that one can remain an evangelical Christian whilst at one and the same time being a Naturist? I am not a contortionist by nature, nor do I believe that one has to become one theologically and scripturally in order to be a Naturist Christian. It seems to me that the more we look into the words, attitudes and concepts that exist within the pages of the Bible and are prepared to take them seriously, the more challenging they become.

Over the years I have come to understand that much of our so-called theology is far from being Biblical. It often owes as much to tradition and culture as it does to the pages of scripture themselves. Many Christians are enculturated into a particular churchmanship with all that it entails and view the bible from those tradition-tinted spectacles which see through a glass darkly.

The true biblical Christian must examine the words in context and seek to draw out the meaning that was intended in the culture in which it was written. That is not to say that God is not at work reinterpreting the scriptures for our present context through the illuminating work of the Holy Spirit for I very much believe that he is. I am simply entering a plea that we take seriously what the Bible has to say to us in as honest and open a way as possible. Tradition does have much to teach us but we always have to ask ourselves the question "When did that tradition arise?" before we stray too far from the biblical tradition in its earliest form.

This book is an attempt to describe my developing understanding, or perhaps my justification for where I am at present. It comes from having been on a pilgrimage of discovery. It is an explanation of my current biblical and theological understanding alongside the other disciplines which inform my current thinking. I hope that each may prove beneficial as others grapple with the feelings, attitudes and understanding that compete and cooperate to make us the unique individuals that God created us to be.

For my wife and our sons

"Love always protects, always trusts, always hopes, always perseveres. Love never fails."

1 Corinthians 13:7,8

CHAPTER 1

A New Beginning

Where should I begin? Where do we begin? We begin in the heart of God and then through the moment at which the twinkle in our parents' eyes precedes that "one flesh" experience. The gametes fuse and weave a new pattern, the pattern is set and the cycle of life begins afresh. Theologians and scientists may debate the moment at which I become a person but the pattern has already been set. Cells divide and multiply, they differentiate, they specialize, the tiny ball of cells takes embryonic form and slowly but surely I am knit together in my mother's womb. Essential nutrients diffuse the umbilicus as I grow and develop in an atmosphere of total dependency. "I am fearfully and wonderfully made," as the Psalmist declares (139:14).

Constrained by my surroundings and expelled through pain and joy, I splutter into a strange new life. These alien surroundings assault my senses until I snuggle at the breast of the one who bore me and the booming beat of my once familiar surroundings is renewed, albeit in a more muted form.

The miracle of new life never ceases to amaze those who are privileged to encounter it. It is essentially a spiritual moment, an experience of awe and wonder, and in essence a glimpse of the glory of God. The naked innocence of the new-born babe reflects the image of God himself if we are at all familiar with the opening chapters of the Bible. "Lets us make human beings in our image ... male and female he created them.... and it was very good."(Gen. 1:26-31)

From that moment of life as we enter the world "born of water" (John 3:5) a whole new set of criteria kick in as we encounter the world in its varied forms and we are moulded by our experience of it. Our relationships with those around us and the sense of the presence or absence of God shape the attitudes and world view which determine our response to every situation. To what extent we react according to nature or nurture has long been debated and no doubt will continue to be.

When Moses was confronted by the burning bush and received his commission from the Lord he demanded to know the name of him who had called him. "I am who I am" or "I will be what I will be" (Ex. 3:14 and footnote) was the response. If only we had the same degree of certainty in the determination of our own identity. The fact is that our self-understanding and our attitudes are in a constant state of flux throughout our lives. We are changed by the circumstances and situations we encounter and it would be strange for anyone to claim that they were the same person after 20 or more years of life experience. Our nature may well be the same but nurture, and our encounter with daily life and environment, cannot fail to have left some impression on the person we think we are.

I suspect many have, in their parents' possession, a photo or two of the "embarrassing" kind which are held back for those special occasions when a prospective partner visits. You know the ones I'm sure. Usually the changing mat with a bare bottom in evidence or even worse the "full frontal" toddler. However, at the time you were not the slightest bit embarrassed. No such thought entered your consciousness; you were simply enjoying the nappy/diaper free experience. If anything you were relieved not to have your movements hindered or were happy for the dreaded nappy rash to be given an airing. In fact most young children are perfectly happy to be running around naked. They have to be taught to dress and certainly the look of relief on a young child's face when they escape the confines of clothing, especially on formal clothing occasions, is an expression of joyful freedom.

Clothing has, until recent years, been an integral part of my life. The human body has both culturally and ecclesiastically been hidden from view, a forbidden area shrouded in fear. In 2005 I found myself unexpectedly on a Naturist/Nudist beach and to cut the proverbial long story short I am now a Naturist/Nudist, at ease with my body and transported back to Eden in my relationship with God.

As a Christian who had personally experienced a powerful work of the Holy Spirit in my life I was accustomed to that "gut feeling" whereby I recognized situations which were not of God. The discernment between right and wrong had always seemed an integral part of my life and yet there in that "shocking" situation everything seemed so right. Somewhat confused, I delved into the Bible re-reading passages that I had read before and noticing that there were a host of passages which spoke of nakedness but not in the supposed condemnatory fashion in which I had previously read them. Let me elaborate......

But first let me clear up a definition. In a recent conversation with a member of my congregation who knew that I was a Naturist she showed me the bird table in her garden and regaled me with the many species that visited it and the wildlife she encountered there. I gently corrected her understanding which she took in her stride and it became apparent that terminology can be confusing. So what is a Naturist/Nudist and what is the difference?

It quickly becomes apparent that it's all a question of geography. In general those in European countries would term themselves naturists and those in the U.S.A. nudists although the terms and understanding might be open to argument. Early in 2009 Fig Leaf Forum, a Naturist Christian online forum, tried to galvanize its world-wide members into producing a definition, and those submitted were then voted upon by the membership. I edited together, what I considered to be the better definitions that others had submitted, and sent in my own version. In the voting that ensued I was surprised to learn that my definition had received most support. It read as follows:-

"Naturism/Nudism is a way of life characterized by the practice of nudity, both alone and in social settings, generally in mixed-gender groups. It encourages self-respect, respect for others and for the environment, embodying freedom and a unique sense of communion with nature. It is purposely non-erotic and non-sexual. A Naturist/Nudist philosophy asserts that the naked human body is inherently decent, and that clothing should not be worn out of shame, but for practical reasons such as warmth, protection and a loving sensitivity to non-naturists/nudists." (Fig Leaf Forum 2009)

The definitions were to be secular in nature, and as a Christian I would want to redefine certain aspects, but for general purposes it works well.

According to the international definition adopted by the XIV Congress of the International Naturist Federation (Agde, France, 1974),

"**Naturism** is: a lifestyle in harmony with nature, expressed through social nudity, and characterised by self-respect of people with different opinions and of the environment."

That version was far more succinct but lacked the breadth and definition of my own version which included those who saw themselves as solitary naturists. Sadly in today's society it was also necessary to include the non-erotic and non-sexual elements to counteract the common misunderstanding that nakedness equates to sex.

CHAPTER 2

Where to now?

My newly found Naturist life has been a rapid journey of discovery, a process whereby I have come to a better realisation of who I am in Christ, and how I reflect his glory in the world. It has been but one strand of the tapestry that is my life. But it has woven its own path alongside the other strands, which have also been interwoven through experience, revelation and faith. In some mysterious way, I can say that "I am who I am" for my life is "hidden with Christ in God" (Col. 3:3). There is a deep satisfaction in that knowledge, for it is the deepest intimacy of relationship for which we were created.

This new journey has been about my body and how it relates to my life in Christ. From the earliest moments of childhood it was hidden away, covered up for fear of being seen: I was tormented through fear of its exposure. The years of puberty were a minefield of myths, about my own body and the bodies of the opposite sex, and reality hardly saw the light of day. The discovery of Christ and new life drew me more and more into that self-discovery and ultimate revelation that I was not only a child of God, but God's glory was revealed in me, even in my body.

I have however, discovered a cunning ploy here. Something that had hitherto remained beyond my consciousness but now seems so blindingly obvious. We were "created in the image of God", are "hidden with Christ in God", and know that "Christ is the image of the invisible God" and yet an unbelieving society has frowned on the public display of that self-same image. "The god of this age has blinded the minds of unbelievers, so that they cannot see the light of the gospel that displays the glory of Christ, who is the image of God." (2 Cor.4:4) More than that, the image has been so distorted that even people of faith believe the "glory" needs to be hidden away; for they too equate it with pornography and an unhealthy sexualisation of that body. Who has won the battle here? Who has so distorted the true image such that bible-believing Christians side with the one, who was so offended with the glory, that he caused it to be hidden away in the garden? "Who told you that you were naked?" (Gen.3:11) asked God, fully knowing the answer.

You may argue that this is confusing the "glory" with the physical body but the incarnation, the entering of God in Jesus into this physical reality of the human body, a second Adam (1 Cor. 15:45), is at least in part about the body. It was that very body in its natural, naked state in which the image of God was first shown its physicality.

Much naturist Christian Theology has centred around the creation account in Genesis, seeing the creation of male and female "in the image of God"(Genesis 1:27) and God's declaration that "it was very good" (v.31) as sufficient reasoning to declare that the existence of the naked body, male and female, was God's creation ordinance. Few would dispute this as the natural created state. However, the debate reaches crisis point when Adam and Eve fall from grace, are banished from Eden, and are clothed by God himself. Does this indicate that the entrance of sin into the world has necessitated the covering of the naked body?

For the naturist Christian in general, the oft cited verse "The man and his wife were both naked, and they felt no shame." (Genesis 2:25) is of critical importance. It may be argued that nakedness and shame are nowhere linked in the scriptures in the sense that the shame is a result of simply being naked. The shame results from the cause of the nakedness whether it be as a result of force, poverty, injustice or immorality. This is particularly evident in having ones assets forcibly removed after conquest. In Isaiah 20:4 we read, "the king of Assyria will lead away stripped and barefoot the Egyptian captives and Cushite exiles, young and old, with buttocks bared - to Egypt's shame." The understanding here is that it is the defeat of Egypt, and the forced removal of all they possess, which is to Egypt's shame. A more complex verse is found in Ezekiel 23:29 "They will deal with you in hatred and take away everything you have worked for. They will leave you stark naked, and the shame of your prostitution will be exposed". The context of the passage talks of plunder with graphical descriptions of the consequences of capture, "They will also strip you of your clothes and take your fine jewellery" (Ezekiel 23:26). Such is the punishment of captives. Note however, that it is the shame of the prostitution, the forsaking of the relationship with God, and not the nakedness, which is condemned. In fact a verse in Job could be said to be an interesting balancing image "Your enemies will be clothed in shame, and the tents of the wicked will be no more." (Job 8:22) This same image of being "clothed in shame" is expressed elsewhere, alongside a similar picture of being "covered with shame" (e.g. Ps. 34:5) and "May my accusers be clothed with disgrace and wrapped in shame as in a cloak." (Ps. 109:29)

There are similar expressions elsewhere including in Isaiah 47 where Babylon is exposed for what she has done and in Nahum 3:5 where the Lord declares "I will lift your skirts over your face. I will show the nations your nakedness and the kingdoms your shame." The clear impression is that of having something done to them against their will.

In human terms the stripping away of all that would prevent us from seeing things as they really are is a powerful image. Jesus declares "let your light shine before others, that they may see your good deeds and glorify your Father in heaven."

(Matthew 5:16) Good things are clearly meant to be seen and not hidden. The light will also illuminate the deeds of the wicked when they are exposed to it. "So let us put aside the deeds of darkness and put on the armour of light" (Romans 13:12).

We live in a society that thrives on exposing political dark deeds that have remained hidden as a result of a "cover up". But have we succumbed to a view of the God-given body as somehow being evil and needing to be covered up? The fact remains that nothing is hidden before God, whether hidden beneath a covering of leaves or hidden behind the lavish robes of royalty. God sees all.

It is fascinating to examine what is really being said, when the Lord God is walking in the garden in Genesis, and shouts out to Adam, "Where are you?" (Genesis 3:9) We can hardly expect God to be unaware of Adam's presence or predicament. It is inconceivable to think that God did not know the whereabouts of Adam. "Where are you?" is not a question of geography but of relationship and position. Other instances of the same Hebrew word "ayeh" which we translate as "where" are to be found in places such as Isaiah 19:12 "Where are your wise men now? Let them show you and make known what the LORD Almighty has planned against Egypt." It is an altogether different sense than the other Hebrew word which we translate as "where", which is used of Joseph when he asks "I'm looking for my brothers. Can you tell me where they are grazing their flocks?" (Genesis 37:16)

It would seem that the real sense of God's question to Adam is more to do with "What's changed?" or "What's different about you?" God is eliciting a confession from Adam, not playing a game of hide and seek. The question lies in the mouth of the counsellor, rather than the cartographer, and Adam's feeble attempt at a literal cover-up fits more with the guilty child, running away to hide from the coming reckoning.

One could still argue that Adam's answer, "I was afraid because I was naked; so I hid" in Genesis 3:10 is a realization that their state of nakedness is no longer appropriate in the new circumstances, however, it is still not a valid argument that nakedness is wrong per se. When God asks the follow-on question, "Who told you that you were naked?" (Gen. 3:11) the obvious implication is that it was not something that came from God, neither was it perceived as a problem. That was precisely how God had created them, interacted with them, and the state in which they had engaged with daily life. It is no surprise that Job could later declare "Naked I came from my mother's womb, and naked I will depart." (Job 1:21) This is part of the natural created order and a simple yet profound realisation that anything else is perhaps superfluous. Jesus, in his sermon on worry points to the flowers of the field, "Consider how the wild flowers grow. They do not labour or spin. Yet I tell you, not even Solomon in all his splendour was dressed like one of these." (Luke 12:27) The body does not need to be clothed to be beautiful. The body is surely splendid simply as it was created, without further adornment. So why does God see fit to clothe Adam and Eve as he banishes them from Eden?

Jewish sages of the Midrash proclaim in the Talmud in Masekhet Sota 14a (juchre.org) that both toward the beginning and toward the end of the Torah, we read of God performing an act of kindness/benevolence for a human being: "R. Simlai expounded: Torah begins with an act of benevolence and ends with an act of benevolence. It begins with an act of benevolence, for it is written: And the Lord God made for Adam and for his wife coats of skin, and clothed them; and it ends with an act of benevolence, for it is written: 'And He buried him in the valley'."

If we are to view the clothing of Adam and Eve as an act of God's kindness as they enter the harsh climate beyond the bounds of Eden it takes upon itself a very different slant from that perceived by the cover-up brigade. God clothes his children to protect them from the thorns and thistles; he equips them to survive the rigours of their new environment, and not because their naked bodies are not fit to see the light of day. This is indeed a gracious act of loving kindness towards his children. He is giving them a fighting chance.

There is another implication here which deserves further study. Much of what is seen in the O.T prefigures the new. There are signs and symbols which point towards a future fulfilment in the life of Jesus. The imperfect prepares us for the perfect which is yet to come in Christ. Might we not see, in the "garments of skin", (Genesis 3:21) the first sacrifice for sin? To provide those garments it would presumably be necessary to shed the blood of animals, an act which would remind them that it was because of their sin that this blood was shed. The difficulty in such conjecture would be that it is not referred to elsewhere in scripture as the prototype sacrifice.

The fact remains that simple nakedness is never condemned in the Bible. Yet there is ample evidence that nakedness was a part of life. There is much said about providing clothing for the naked which leads us to believe that there were indeed people who were naked. This is never said in a condemnatory fashion but out of compassion. "If you take your neighbour's cloak as a pledge, return it by sunset, because that cloak is the only covering your neighbour has. What else can your neighbour sleep in? When he cries out to me, I will hear, for I am compassionate." (Exodus 22:26,27) Alongside similar passages the impression given is that the poor only possessed a single precious garment which served a multitude of purposes. Poverty and nakedness went hand in hand as a fact of life. Having personally experienced frost and ice on the temple mount in Jerusalem the necessity of clothing the poor becomes obvious. It is also self-evident that as clothing was used as a pledge, people lived in a state of nakedness until that clothing was redeemed.

There are also some fascinating passages of scripture where nakedness may be seen as the command of God and the action of the Spirit of God. In Isaiah chapter 20:2 we read how God commanded Isaiah to "Take off the sackcloth from your body and the sandals from your feet." And he did so, going around stripped and barefoot." The context quite clearly indicates that Isaiah lived naked for three years as a prophetic sign against Egypt. Can we envisage a situation where God actually commands someone to do something which is deemed to be sinful? Such a view does not fit with the character and action of God in the biblical account. For Isaiah it would certainly be uncomfortable, but not sinful.

In 1 Samuel 19:24 we read how "He (Saul) stripped off his garments, and he too prophesied in Samuel's presence. He lay naked all that day and all that night. This is why people say, "Is Saul also among the prophets?" The indication is that the bands of prophets were characterized by their nakedness. No further explanation is given, but it may be similarly argued that when David danced before the Lord with all his might, as he led the procession of the Ark of the Covenant up to Jerusalem, his state of undress was the work of the Spirit as well. Nowhere is this specified, and neither was David completely naked, for he was wearing a linen ephod, but his actions precipitated the following rebuke from his wife Michal, "How the king of Israel has distinguished himself today, going around half-naked in full view of the slave girls of his servants as any vulgar fellow would!" (2 Samuel 6:20) Simply wearing a linen ephod, a light garment reaching from the breast to the hip, would have left nothing to the imagination.

Michal's disgust only served to earn her a rebuke from David and the final verse states that she had no children to the day of her death. We are given no indication as to whether this was God's punishment upon her or simply that David never slept with her again. Both are distinct possibilities. We are left with the comparison of the king to "any vulgar fellow", implying that such behaviour was beneath his dignity, or further reinforcing the fact that the common folk were often seen naked. Following on from previous comments, it is a commonly held view that labourers laboured naked, both in the fields and elsewhere. Post Maccabean rabbinical thought does apply itself to the issue of nakedness. Michael L. Satlow in his paper on "Jewish constructions of nakedness", points out the ways in which it was deemed proper to cover the male genitals in Jewish worship accepting that nakedness was part of life in those times. There is a description of a legal sanction in Deuteronomy 25:11 whereby "If two men are fighting and the wife of one of them comes to rescue her husband from his assailant, and she reaches out and seizes him by his private parts," then she should have her hand cut off. The very fact that she is able to do that insinuates that a degree of nakedness was involved. The sanction is related to issues of the sanctity of life and the generation of offspring.

Peter was fishing naked in Galilee in the post resurrection appearance in John 21. The greek word "gymnos" is used which literally means naked although some modern translations appear to be a little squeamish in translating that word (see Matthew Neal).

Another incidence of nakedness is that of the young man in Gethsemane. "A young man, wearing nothing but a linen garment, was following Jesus. When they seized him, he fled naked, leaving his garment behind." (Mark 14:51,52) The young man is commonly identified as the author of the gospel, hence the inclusion of the incident, but it gives further indication that the dress code was such, there being no concept of underwear as we know it, except for priests in their ritual duties. We are reminded of another incident in Genesis 39:12 where Joseph fled the scene of the sexual advances of Potiphar's wife and "he left his cloak in her hand and ran out of the house." Again there is no indication that he was naked although there is much argument that he was.

There is archaeological evidence that there was often little clothing evidenced in ancient Egypt, including tablets found at Tel-el-Amarna in 1887 detailing the situation of Pharoah Akhen-Aton and his queen Nefertiti . In a society which worshipped Aton the Sun God, "not only the Pharaoh and his wife but also their children and officials went around with too few clothes (transparent at that!) or no clothes at all, that they practiced nudity in the royal palace, in the royal gardens and swimming pool". (Aileen Goodson.) These snippets of background information perhaps give us some indication of the state of dress or undress of Egyptian society, although we need to remember that particular robes indicated status and authority. In that context we can draw parallels with the robe given to Joseph by his father Jacob in Genesis 37:3 "Now Israel loved Joseph more than any of his other sons, because he had been born to him in his old age; and he made a richly ornamented robe for him." The resultant furore within the family, and subsequent events, support the understanding that garments conferred status in the Hebrew culture as well.

At this point it is interesting to note the special requirement of particular garments for priests for their cultic duties. Exodus 20:26 is another fascinating passage which many use as an argument against nakedness, "do not go up to my altar on steps, lest your nakedness be exposed on it." There is nothing here to indicate the rationale behind the phrase but it is not linked with any moral argument and may simply be a practice which distinguished Hebrew worship practices from the surrounding nations, and the fertility cults which were prevalent in those societies.

The specifications for ceremonial robes for worship in the tabernacle include the following verse, "Make linen undergarments as a covering for the body, reaching from the waist to the thigh. Aaron and his sons must wear them whenever they enter the Tent of Meeting or approach the altar to minister in the Holy Place, so that they will not incur guilt and die." (Exodus 28:42-43) This is one of only a few references to underwear and, as elsewhere, is only required of the priests in the performance of their duties. The threat of death, if such commands are not adhered to, is equally applied to any failure to ceremonially wash hands and feet. Guilt is incurred whenever the Lords instructions are not adhered to. The specific garments for the priests were both symbolic and indicative of their status. The putting on and removal of clothing appears to be part of the ceremonial regulations e.g. Leviticus 6:10,11 "The priest shall then put on his linen clothes, with linen undergarments next to his body, and shall remove the ashes of the burnt offering that the fire has consumed on the altar and place them beside the altar. Then he is to take off these clothes and put on others, and carry the ashes outside the camp to a place that is ceremonially clean." We are left with the impression here that this clothing is put on and removed in the same way as present day coveralls, for protection and cleanliness. The very fact that this ceremonial underwear was prescribed indicates that underwear was not the normal dress code. Elsewhere, in the ordination ceremony of Aaron and his sons, we see instructions for Moses to ceremonially wash them before clothing them with their priestly robes. The presumably public spectacle of this ceremony would indicate once again that nudity in itself was not frowned upon in biblical society.

Another aspect of priestly life was the examination of the skin of the people with regard to infectious skin diseases such as those prescribed in Leviticus 13. Much as a doctor would today examine one's body in the diagnosing of disease, so the priests would examine the bodies of the people to declare them ritually clean or unclean. It can hardly be argued that they would have remained clothed during this examination. Nevertheless, we may not assume that this event was any more public than any doctor's surgery today although there is no prescription, in the otherwise detailed legal formularies, that this should be done in private. In fact the whole point was that the designation of a person as ritually clean or unclean was a public declaration. Whether this was a visual demonstration or simply a priestly announcement remains unspecified.

CHAPTER 3

A sign of the Covenant

We cannot look at the issue of our bodies and faith without some consideration of the issue of circumcision. The removal of the foreskin of the male penis, as a sign of the covenant between God and Abraham, was Abraham's response of agreement to the promises of God. God declared in Genesis 17:11 "You are to undergo circumcision, and it will be the sign of the covenant between me and you" and he went on to say that this would be an everlasting sign of that covenant, "for the generations to come." (v.12) It was to be performed upon every male child eight days after birth, and also upon every male slave or servant who was purchased into the household. Those who belonged to God's chosen people were to demonstrate that belonging by the outward and visible sign of circumcision. The focus here is on that outward visible sign.

In order to fulfil its purpose the sign of circumcision must have been regularly visible. As previously mentioned, nakedness was such an ordinary part of everyday life for the ancient people of God that their identity, through circumcision, was never in doubt. Through ceremonial washing and bathing at the very least, and working on the land and the shared household living of most people, there would not have been an opportunity to keep one's identity hidden. In Acts 16 we read how Paul had Timothy circumcised before taking him along on one of his journeys. Paul did not want Timothy's uncircumcised state to detract from sharing the gospel. Such an act would have been unnecessary if the penis was covered and hidden. Daily life must have given rise to communal nakedness such that their belonging through circumcision was never in doubt.

The fact is that the Jew would have prided himself on his circumcision. It would have set him apart as one of God's chosen people. To his mind there were only two types of people, the circumcised and the uncircumcised and he would never have wanted to be identified with the latter. That said, it must also be recognised that there were times when circumcision lapsed, like the occasion where those who had been born during the wilderness wanderings had not been circumcised. God said to Joshua, "Make flint knives and circumcise the Israelites again." And later explains the situation (Joshua 5:2). There was also a particular period during inter-testamental times under the rule of Antiochus Epiphanes that some Jews "built a gymnasium in Jerusalem, according to Gentile custom, and removed the marks of circumcision, and abandoned the holy covenant." (1 Maccabees 1:14-15) Whether this equated to some crude kind of plastic surgery we may only speculate. The purpose was to fit in with Greek society especially in the gymnasium, which was literally a place where people exercised, bathed and philosophised naked ("gymnos" means "naked".) Such actions would have alienated them from God's faithful people and helped precipitate the Maccabean revolts to re-establish the faith and nation of Israel.

It is perhaps a further indication of the prudish nature of the modern day church that the issue of circumcision is hardly discussed. Most Christians in British and North American churches would be embarrassed to discuss issues of such a nature. They would be quickly glossed over, to the point that many would be ignorant of what circumcision actually entailed.

At this point we cannot avoid the fact that Jesus himself was circumcised (Luke 2:21). He belonged to the society described above and was thoroughly immersed in that culture. Incarnation is literally "in the flesh" and he nowhere alludes to any need to hide that self-same flesh from others. His circumcision would have been as visible as any other Jew. He would have fed at the bare breast of his mother as any other child.

Many argue that Jesus was baptized naked by John the Baptist in the River Jordan. Ceremonial washings and ritual bathing were performed naked and by full immersion as every part of the body needed to be in contact with the water (according to Nishmat: The Jerusalem Center for Advanced Jewish Study for Women, even bandages and stitches may have to be removed during ritual bathing). The water is meant to be running water, referred to as "living water", hence the symbolic statement by Jesus in John chapter 4 about giving living water to the Samaritan woman at the well, an allusion to a ritual cleansing which she is in need of, as Jesus refers to her lifestyle later in the passage.

A Jewish ritual bath or mikveh is used:

- by Jewish women to achieve ritual purity after menstruation or childbirth

- by Jewish men to achieve ritual purity

- as part of a traditional procedure for conversion to Judaism

The Baptism for repentance administered by John is generally understood to be a ritual washing equivalent to the procedure undertaken by Gentiles converting to Judaism (T.F. Torrance, "Proselyte Baptism" NTS 1 (1954), 150-154). The point here is that it was a public event and those undergoing the ritual were naked. This demonstrates that nudity in matters of faith was not an issue in biblical times, it was a natural part of the culture of the day.

At this point it may be useful to delve into early Christian history to ascertain whether such practices were carried on into the life of the church. Early Christian images from the catacombs illustrating baptism often indicated that the person being baptized was naked eg. the fresco in the crypt of Lucina c.100A.D. and the fresco in the Gallery of the Sacraments in S. Callistus c.200A.D. (Driver p.239 ff.) Along with early accounts of Christian rites of baptism it seems that nudity was not an option: it was a requirement of the church. Cyril of Jerusalem, 4th century, wrote of the procedure for baptism as follows;

"As soon, then, as ye entered, ye put off your tunic; and this was an image of putting off the old man with his deeds. Having stripped yourselves, ye were naked; in this also imitating Christ, who was stripped naked on the Cross, and by His nakedness put off from Himself the principalities and powers, and openly triumphed over them on the tree." This was part of a lecture on "The Mysteries of Baptism" (Jerusalem, S. C.). He goes on to declare, "O wondrous thing! ye were naked in the sight of all, and were not ashamed; " (All "persons were baptized naked, either in imitation of Adam in Paradise, or our Saviour upon the Cross, or to signify their putting off the body of sin, and the old man with his deeds.") "for truly ye bore the likeness of the first-formed Adam, who was naked in the garden, and was not ashamed."

Another early father of the church Hippolytus, in the 3rd century, also refers to the practice of baptising the candidates naked, "They shall remove their clothing. And first baptize the little ones; if they can speak for themselves, they shall do so; if not, their parents or other relatives shall speak for them. Then baptize the men, and last of all the women; they must first loosen their hair and put aside any gold or silver ornaments that they were wearing: let no one take any alien thing down to the water with them." (Hippolytus) Note the similarities with the ritual Jewish mikveh and the removal of every item. He then describes the candidates standing naked in the water for the act of baptism itself. Such early references would seem to support the continuation of the New Testament tradition.

It would seem to imply from this material that Baptismal tradition has changed through the history of the church according to changing culture. If we were to appeal to the earliest traditions, as best representing the faith and practice of the church closest to its source, then we would have a strong case that naked baptism by immersion best represents the symbolic practices of the early church.

It was mentioned in the liturgical practices above that naked baptism was deemed to be symbolic of a return to Adam's original state, through the forgiveness of sins and the new life in Christ. This is indeed a powerful symbol and an argument for the pure state of nudity. One might argue that this would preclude non-Christians from appearing in the same state as they had not attained the same state of innocence, however, the underlying argument still holds that it is cultural attitudes which determine our state of dress or undress. There is strong theological symbolism in being naked before God but that does not detract from the underlying issue which is the attitude of the heart. We shall return to that argument shortly.

CHAPTER 4

What did Jesus do?

The common appeal to conscience in the modern church is often "What would Jesus do?" WWJD as the wristbands and necklaces remind us These re-inventions of the phylacteries of old are a reminder that it is the practice of Jesus, the inaugurator of the New Covenant, which informs our Christian understanding. His words, recorded in the gospels and interpreted by his actions are key to our understanding of the issues which inform our life and practice. These are further unpacked in the epistles, whereby the early practitioners of the faith seek to pass on to the next generation of believers how we should live out the faith in everyday life. We cannot avoid the fact that nearly two thousand years have passed since these were recorded and we live in a culture which is vastly different from that in which they were first interpreted. We read these ancient documents in the light of our own culture and tradition.

If we are at all able to read afresh these self-same documents from a different cultural perspective some things might leap out at us from the pages which were culturally invisible before. If we are, for a moment, to accept some of the assertions made in previous chapters, about the non-issue of cultural nakedness in the everyday life of biblical society, some things seem to make sense.

In a very matter of fact way, and more informed by movies than the scriptures, we previously understood Jesus to have some kind of loincloth or such as he hung on the cross. Perhaps he was wearing a nappy to hide the fact that he would wet himself and defecate during the trauma of crucifixion? The scriptures inform us that the soldiers gambled for his garments and John gives us the most elaborate description of what took place, "When the soldiers crucified Jesus, they took his clothes, dividing them into four shares, one for each of them, with the undergarment remaining. This garment was seamless, woven in one piece from top to bottom. "Let's not tear it," they said to one another. "Let's decide by lot who will get it." This happened that the scripture might be fulfilled that said, "They divided my clothes among them and cast lots for my garment." So this is what the soldiers did." (John 19:23.24) The understanding is that his outer robe was torn into strips of material along the seams, which they would be able to sell. Such garments would have been constructed from various pieces of material and were of sufficient value that they could be left as collateral against debt, as we have already seen. A seamless single piece of material was best kept intact. This was his undergarment. There would have been no further garment to preserve his dignity. Jesus would have been crucified naked. The Jewish identity of the "King of the Jews" would have been clearly displayed for all to see. But dignity as understood by our culture is not the same as first century dignity. The indignity and shame of the cross is not because of the nakedness per se but because of the ritual humiliation of being forcibly stripped of all possessions and executed as a criminal with the intense pain causing the involuntary emptying of the bowels as an added humiliation. However, the real indignity is the innocent victim, castigated as a law-breaker, with the shame of our sin upon his shoulders. The shame was the sin which he bore upon the cross as a covering; a covering which cut him off from his Father in heaven. "My God, my God, why have you forsaken me?" (Matthew 27:46)

At the point of death we are told by Matthew that, "the tombs broke open. The bodies of many holy people who had died were raised to life." (Matthew 27:52) Should we be led to believe that they were miraculously clothed at the same time?

I think not. This brings us to the state of the resurrected body of Jesus.

The body was "wrapped in linen cloth" and hurriedly placed in the tomb. The women went away to prepare spices and perfumes with which to anoint the body following the Sabbath. When the tomb was found to be empty following the Sabbath it was Peter who entered the tomb and "saw the strips of linen lying by themselves." (Luke 24:12) In John's gospel we have even more description of how "he saw the strips of linen lying there, as well as the cloth that had been wrapped around Jesus' head. The cloth was still lying in its place, separate from the linen."(John 20:6,7) The plain fact was that the body was missing, and any form of covering that had been in place had been left behind. The resurrected Jesus was naked.

John goes on to describe the incident where Mary is sat weeping outside the tomb and mistakes the risen Jesus for the gardener. One simple explanation sheds light on the reason she probably mistook him for a gardener. We have previously described a culture where labourers were prone to work without their garments. A naked Jesus would have fitted this category perfectly. He was hardly likely to be a Roman guard or even a religious official without their garments of office. If we look further to the resurrection appearances of Jesus to his disciples behind closed doors we may note the fact that "he showed them his hands and side." (John 20:20) They saw the marks of the nails and the wound in his side and believed. A week later he appeared again with Thomas present, "Then he said to Thomas, "Put your finger here; see my hands. Reach out your hand and put it into my side. Stop doubting and believe." (John 20:27) The most logical explanation for the possibility of such an act being able to take place was that the risen Jesus was naked. "Even Solomon in all his splendour" (Luke 12:27) would not have had the glory of the risen Jesus.

CHAPTER 5

Concrete objections?

I hope that I have not avoided or glossed over some of the scriptural objections that are wheeled out in defence of a strict dress code. There are both passages of scripture and quotations from the early Fathers which might be read as objections to the human body being seen naked.

One of the most quoted is the incident in which Noah in Genesis 9:21ff "became drunk and lay uncovered inside his tent. Ham, the father of Canaan, saw his father's nakedness and told his two brothers outside. But Shem and Japheth took a garment and laid it across their shoulders; then they walked in backward and covered their father's nakedness." When Noah awoke and discovered what had happened he cursed Canaan for what his father Ham had done. This passage has been argued over by many scholars such that Professor R Davidson in his commentary on the passage states that, "It has been well said that this passage is 'filled with difficulties and obscurities for which the final word has not been spoken.'"

Steven Greenberg argues from the Talmudic literature that the incident is about more than what lies at face value. He comments that the rabbis "Rav and Shmuel (disagreed). One said he [Ham] castrated him [Noah] and the other said he raped him". The argument is that whatever it was, it was so serious that it entailed the curse of Canaan, Ham's son. It is beyond belief that this was simply gazing upon someone who was naked, or even making fun of that fact. The rabbinical arguments seem to make the most logical argument for the incident, that some degree of sexual impropriety had taken place. The jury is still out on that one.

Leviticus 18 contains a whole series of verses which are commonly used to combat nakedness by the repeat use of the phrase "You shall not uncover the nakedness of...", followed by a particular person or even animal. However, that phrase, which in this case I have quoted from the NRSV, is translated as "Do not have sexual relations with... "in the TNIV which, in the context, is a far more apt living translation of what is deemed to be a euphemism in the original rendering.

Revelation chapter 3:17ff declares, "You say, 'I am rich; I have acquired wealth and do not need a thing.' But you do not realize that you are wretched, pitiful, poor, blind and naked. I counsel you to buy from me gold refined in the fire, so you can become rich; and white clothes to wear, so you can cover your shameful nakedness; and salve to put on your eyes, so you can see." Again the context requires us to examine the meaning and not to take the words at face value. Revelation, by its very nature as apocalyptic literature, is full of figurative and symbolic language and we are required to draw away the veil to understand what is actually being said.

The picture is the assumption that the worldly treasure of those being condemned has left them devoid of spiritual treasure. The images of being naked when they believe themselves to be dressed in fine apparel and blind when they believe themselves to be seeing clearly are obviously metaphorical. Neither blindness nor nakedness are being condemned here as some kind of moral evil. The very fact that they are required to buy gold, white robes and salve as the antidote to their predicament, when they already see themselves as possessing these very things, surely tells us that what is required is a spiritual and virtuous transformation of their lives. The answer is definitely not a trip to the bank, the tailors, and the local opticians.

Revelation 16:15 "Look, I come like a thief! Blessed are those who stay awake and keep their clothes on, so that they may not go naked and be shamefully exposed," presents us with a similar quandary. To interpret it literally would require us to be clothed at all times and never to sleep. FF Bruce in his commentary notes that "according to the Mishnah, the captain of the temple in Jerusalem went his rounds of the precincts by night, and if a member of the temple police was caught asleep at his post, his clothes were taken off and burned, and he was sent away naked in disgrace" (Howley & F. F. Bruce p.657,) The picture is simply that of being prepared, as in the readiness to leave Egypt at the Passover "with your cloak tucked into your belt, your sandals on your feet and your staff in your hand." (Exodus 12:11). To be asleep naked, as was the nightly state, would have been shameful if you were required to be ready for immediate action. When Peter was in prison the angel told him to "Put on your clothes and sandals." And Peter did so. "Wrap your cloak around you and follow me," he said. (Acts 12:8) We may surmise that he is sleeping naked.

James in chapter 2 of his letter writes "Suppose a brother or sister is without clothes and daily food. If one of you says to them, "Go in peace; keep warm and well fed," but does nothing about their physical needs, what good is it? (James 2:15,16) There is no reference here to anything except satisfying a simple physical need. We need read nothing further into the text. Paul advises Timothy (1 Timothy 2:9,10) that "I also want the women to dress modestly, with decency and propriety, adorning themselves, not with elaborate hairstyles or gold or pearls or expensive clothes, but with good deeds, appropriate for women who profess to worship God." If we are to interpret this as a requirement to dress we may similarly define the state of dress to be solely with good deeds.

In the light of our previous argument about the naked state of the resurrected Christ we have a fascinating argument as to our clothing requirement if we are to be clothed with Christ

(Galatians 3:27) and in 2 Corinthians 5 to be "clothed with our heavenly dwelling", which is our imperishable spiritual body.

On a different tangent we also may wish to join others in arguing that when Jesus "got up from the meal, took off his outer clothing, and wrapped a towel around his waist" at the last supper (John 13:4), he washed their feet whilst being naked. The designation "outer garment" in the TNIV is a mistranslation of the Greek word "ἱμάτια" which is better translated as garments, or clothes. This is the same plural word employed by John in chapter 19:23 when the soldiers gambled for Jesus' clothes. This argument of translation is forwarded by Leon Morris in his footnote on the verse.

At this point it may well be argued that that Jesus was not naked as he had a towel "around his waist" but again the Greek is unclear on this. To dry feet with a towel tightly wound around the waist would prove to be somewhat difficult. To have the towel draped over his shoulders would make more sense. The Greek word "διαζώννυμι" is only used in two places in the New Testament, the other being the description of Peter putting on his fishers garment when he leapt into the lake in the resurrection appearance in John 21. Again the translation in context would make more sense if the towel/coat was across the shoulders. See Matthew Neal "Squeamish translating Part 2" for a more detailed argument.

When reading some of the early Fathers of the church we have already seen some comments on Baptismal practice. St. Cyprien in his treatise "On the dress of Virgins" declares, "But what of those who frequent promiscuous baths; who prostitute to eyes that are curious to lust, bodies that are dedicated to chastity and modesty? They who disgracefully behold naked men, and are seen naked by men, do they not themselves afford enticement to vice, do they not solicit and invite the desires of those present to their own corruption and wrong?" At first sight we have a clear prohibition on mixed sex nudity, however the baths concerned are clearly designated "promiscuous" and the later description appears to describe the said virgins as making a deliberate show of their bodies "to be pointed at and to be handled."(II:14). Furthermore in the next sentence he denigrates cosmetic adornment saying "the work of God and His fashioning and formation ought in no manner to be adulterated, either with the application of yellow colour, or with black dust or rouge, or with any kind of medicament which can corrupt the native lineaments. God says, "Let us make man in our image and likeness;" Gen.1:26 and does anyone dare to alter and to change what God has made? They are laying hands on God when they try to re-form that which He formed, and to transfigure it, not knowing that everything which comes into being is God's work, everything that is changed is the devil's" (II:15)

"Having put on silk and purple, they cannot put on Christ; adorned with gold, and pearls, and necklaces, they have lost the ornaments of the heart and spirit." (II:13) We are challenged to examine those attitudes of heart and spirit at every step of our walk with God and it is perhaps here that we approach a crucial matter.

Jesus declares quite plainly (Mark 7:18-23) "Don't you see that nothing that enters you from the outside can defile you? For it doesn't go into your heart but into your stomach, and then out of your body." (In saying this, Jesus declared all foods clean.) He went on: "What comes out of you is what defiles you. For from within, out of your hearts, come evil thoughts, sexual immorality, theft, murder, adultery, greed, malice, deceit, lewdness, envy, slander, arrogance and folly. All these evils come from inside and defile you." Although the argument is primarily related to food it equally applies to other situations as well. Thus it could be said that simple non-sexual nudity cannot defile us at its face value. It is the attitude in which such conduct is exercised which lies at the heart of it being right or wrong.

Paul applies a similar argument in Romans 14:13-23 relating to food regulations. I took the liberty of reworking the passage in a document I submitted to the "Naturist Christian" online forum. I simply took the sentiments expressed and applied them in the following way,

> "[13] Therefore let us stop passing judgment on one another. Instead, make up your mind not to put any stumbling block or obstacle in the way of a brother or sister. [14] I am convinced, being fully persuaded in the Lord Jesus, that nakedness is not unclean in itself. But if anyone regards nakedness as unclean, then for that person it is unclean. [15] If your brother or sister is distressed by your nakedness, you are no longer acting in love. Do not by promoting your nakedness destroy your brother or sister for whom Christ died. [16] Therefore do not let what you know is good be spoken of as evil. [17] For the kingdom of God is not a matter of being clothed or unclothed, but of righteousness, peace and joy in the Holy Spirit, [18] because anyone who serves Christ in this way is pleasing to God and receives human approval.
>
> [19] Let us therefore make every effort to do what leads to peace and to mutual edification. [20] Do not destroy the work of God for the sake of nakedness. Nakedness is clean, but it is wrong for a person to parade their nakedness if that causes someone else to stumble. [21] It is better not to be naked or to do anything else that will cause your brother or sister to fall.

[22] So whatever you believe about these things keep between yourself and God. Blessed are those who do not condemn themselves by what they approve. [23] But those who have doubts are condemned if they are naked before others, if their nakedness is not from faith; and everything that does not come from faith is sin."

I contend that the above reworking of the passage is a legitimate attempt to apply Christian principles to the topic under discussion and I would summarize my position as follows, "I am convinced, being fully persuaded in the Lord Jesus, that nakedness is not unclean in itself." (v.14 above). In the same vein I recognise that there are many who will remain unconvinced by the arguments I have put forward. I also recognise that of themselves many of the scriptural arguments are open to alternative interpretation.

Much of my scriptural evidence is circumstantial. The fact is that the bible is largely silent on the matter. Nakedness is neither condemned nor promoted and nowhere is it described as being sinful: we are left to make up our own minds. In the process I hope that our appreciation of the human body as the pinnacle of God's creation and its significance in reflecting the image of God and making him known is recognised "For now we see only a reflection as in a mirror; then we shall see face to face. Now I know in part; then I shall know fully, even as I am fully known." (1 Corinthians 12:12)

Alongside this I recognise that "just as we have borne the image of the earthly man, so shall we bear the image of the heavenly man" (1 Corinthians 15:49) and my "natural body" will be raised a "spiritual body" (see v.44). The point is that we should not reject or ignore our bodies, no matter how imperfect we perceive them to be. They are important to God and are his gift to us. A simple word search for "body" in the New Testament reveals a wealth of imagery to illuminate our understanding of the importance of our bodies and the right use of the same. Such arguments contend against the dualistic philosophies of the Gnostic sects which attempted to undermine early Christianity and against which John wrote his first letter. (Andrew Farley)

"Every spirit that acknowledges that Jesus Christ has come in the flesh is from God," (1 John 4:2) John purposefully promotes the physical and lays stress on the fleshly physical nature of Jesus to counteract the "purely spiritual" claims of Gnosticism. Sadly much of modern Christianity seems to have fallen into a Gnostic dualism when it comes to valuing the very bodies that God created "naked" and "very good". Most churches concentrate on the spiritual aspect of our faith and are happy to engage with the physical when it comes to engaging with poverty, sickness and community needs. However, that does not stretch to engaging with the body itself in its naked physical form.

The preoccupation of society with sex and pornography when it comes to the nude form has precipitated a reflex response from the church to cover up. This is particularly noticeable in relation to female fashion. There are articles on the internet debating the length of skirts, the need to hide cleavage, and whether or not it is right for Christian women to wear a bikini. The protection of Christians from society's misuse and abuse of the human form is to hide away the body instead of confronting the attitudes and wrong thinking which pervade much of society. Surely this kind of response is simply conceding the battle and even reinforcing such views by a prudish conservative response. Perhaps the Spirit is challenging the church to reclaim the lost image and speak prophetically to this false conditioning of our society. Perhaps the Lord is calling for new Isaiah's to stand naked and proclaim God's judgement against those who seek to despoil his image in the very bodies he created to glorify that self-same image.

CHAPTER 6

But is it art?

Art is perhaps one of the media which has best incorporated an honest view of the human body into its repertoire. To venture into an art gallery of any stature and not to be confronted with the naked form would be a rarity. Art takes many forms but the visual arts have always sought to portray the human body in a variety of ways. It is not immune from contextualisation particularly when the artist has to earn a living. Popular art has always pandered to the preferences of the day and in that sense can give us an insight into the culture in which it was produced. At the same time the avant garde movements have often sought to break new ground and educate those same societies into a new appreciation of their surroundings. The glossary on the Tate Gallery website declares it to be "that which is in the forefront, is innovatory, which introduces and explores new forms and in some cases new subject matter."

The church has always sought to share the faith through its use of imagery. It has portrayed the life of Christ and the content of the bible in a visual way since early times, particularly during those periods of history where populations were largely illiterate. As literacy rates have improved I would venture that the art forms have shifted away from mere storytelling towards being thought provoking in true avant garde nature.

The nude male form is very evident in classical Greek sculpture (Osborne R.) especially in the portrayal of the gods and heroes of antiquity. Today there has been a culture shift towards a predominantly female portrayal of the nude body for which I will leave the reasoning to others.

There has been considerable portrayal of the naked body in art which depicts Christian themes particularly from earlier times. I have previously referred to naked baptismal images found in the catacombs but through different periods of history the church has invoked censorship according to the religious culture of the day. It may be argued that some of these movements were responses to the excesses of the day, equivalent to the "fashion cover up" invoked by conservative evangelical churches today.

One of the most striking of these movements occurred during the Renaissance where, following the Council of Trent, many artworks were altered to hide the genital areas. This was particularly noticeable in the Vatican's Sistine Chapel where the artist Daniele da Volterra was commissioned to cover the genital areas which earned him the historical nickname "Il Braghettone", the breeches-painter. (Michaelangelo)

One fascinating example of a cover-up was that done to the fresco "The Expulsion from the Garden of Eden", by Masaccio in a church in Florence. It was painted in 1425, then in 1680 some vines were strategically painted over the genital areas. The painting was restored to its former naked condition in 1980. A classical nude sculpture is Michelangelo's "David" which conveys another account of censorship. A copy of the statue was presented to Queen Victoria in 1857 which has given rise to a modern day exhibition in the Victoria and Albert museum surrounding a large plaster fig leaf which was used to hide the genitals when female dignitaries were passing. (David's Fig Leaf)

I make reference to the above material to illustrate the argument that it is the cultural attitudes which have changed over history, to the point that what passed for innocent portrayal in earlier years could subsequently be deemed immoral or even pornographic in later times. It is for us to reason as to whether this is a healthy situation or a sign of the moral degradation of society's attitude toward what should be God's greatest masterpiece.

CHAPTER 7

Brave Nude World

Our present culture is in the midst of huge changes both in terms of community, morality, politics, technology and much more beside. There are a host of movements with conflicting ideals battling for the heart of society at large. Organisations like the Christian Naturist Fellowship have the following aims:-

To:

Provide a meeting place and forum in which Christians, who enjoy appropriate clothing free places and activities, can support and encourage each other.

Help Christians within Naturism to study the Bible for themselves and to reconcile their Faith with their Naturism.

Encourage Christians within Naturism to share their Faith with their fellow Naturists.

Provide answers to Naturists interested in finding out how Christ is relevant to their lives today.

On the other hand there are Christians who campaign to have any expression of public nakedness banned, such as Portsmouth Family Church who ran a campaign in September 2011 to petition the government to change the law on public expressions of nudity such as the World Naked Bike Ride.

It is hardly surprising that there are theological disagreements between different elements of the church. Differences have been expressed since the earliest days of the church with factions vying for legitimacy. The apostle Paul broke company from some of his fellow travellers (Acts 15:39) and castigated Peter (Galatians 2:11). There was a Council at Jerusalem to sort out disagreements in the church (Acts 15). Paul was at great pains to try and heal the divisions that existed in the church at Corinth. Is it any wonder that after two thousand years the situation has not improved?

In relation to Naturism, it is hardly surprising that the response quoted earlier, surrounding my Cathedral controversy, that "The Church of England said it had no official policy on naturism," could be because the defining of a policy would likely spark further controversy. However, we must always keep in mind that our Lord Jesus Christ never shied away from controversy himself, even when it came from those who were seen as the guardians of the faith.

There is an oft quoted article by Pope John Paul II whist he was still Karol Wojtyla which states that, "There are circumstances where nakedness is not immodest..... Immodesty is present only when nakedness plays a negative role with regard to the value of the person," (Karol Wojtyla, p.190). This is a passage that many Roman Catholic naturists take to heart as validation of their lifestyle by the church. It is to be hoped that if churches were to actually spend some time getting to grips with the theological issues surrounding Naturism then at the very least there would be some well-informed discussion rather than knee-jerk reactions.

What of the world in all this? From my own observations of the world, public expressions of nudity have become ever more popular. More organisations are producing "Calendar Girls" style calendars to raise funds, following the ever popular account of the nude calendar produced by a Womens Institute in Yorkshire in 1999 which was subsequently portrayed very successfully in the cinema. Dramatic Societies are producing their own versions of the "Full Monty", another cinema hit with a male striptease as its subject. TV documentaries and reality shows venture into naked portrayals.

The question to be asked is why are such shows produced and what is the reasoning behind them? Are many of these produced simply to elevate the viewing figures through titillation rather than information?

There are also some fine examples of television demonstrating the positive effects of naturism. Although not a "naturist" programme, Gok Wan's "How to look good naked" has shown how poor body image can be sensitively addressed through a process of affirmation and encouragement. The benefits, particularly in terms of increased self-confidence, are noticeable, and follow on programmes, where the participants are contacted sometime after the show, seem to demonstrate a lasting effect. The series "The Naked Office" in which business consultant Seven Suphi attempted to improve the success of a variety of businesses through a series of team building exercise's, culminating in a "naked as you dare" day in the office, similarly appeared to have lasting beneficial effects on the companies involved.

Another programme "Trinny and Susannah Undress the Nation" on ITV in 2007 focussed again on body image and some episodes, where nudity was involved before the broadcasting watershed, attracted objections. An ITV spokesman commented "The context of this programme fully justified the use of footage of women topless and in bras. The presenters were pursuing a serious subject in an engaging and entertaining way." ("What not to bare", London Evening Standard 2008) The content was justifiable in terms of the subject matter but one may be led to question what constitutes "engaging and entertaining". All too often nudity is sexualised and poked fun at, often provoking nervous giggling through the perceived embarrassment of the viewing public and further perpetuating the "naughty" myth.

It is difficult to find any programmes which involve nudity being treated in an objective way. One of the better examples was a programme first broadcast in September 2011 on BBC Three entitled "Cherry's Body Dilemmas". The BBC blog for the programme described it as follows, "Cherry Healey is a slave to her bathroom scales. As her teenage diaries reveal, diets and looking thin has been a lifelong obsession. And with 37 per cent of women in the UK on a diet 'most or all of the time', she's not alone. Now Cherry wants to tackle her body neurosis, so she meets up with women of all shapes and sizes to find out what makes a body beautiful. From a bodybuilder to a fat and happy fashionista, from a nudist to a frustrated slimmer, Cherry takes a look at women's body hang-ups to see if she can get rid of her own demons once and for all." (BBC ,Sept 2011)

The programme was well put together, if not frightening in its content. The poor state of women's body image was explored from a wide variety of perspectives beginning from that of the presenter herself. It was somewhat distressing to see young women who were dissatisfied with their bodies to the extent that they were considering cosmetic surgery. These were looked at from different cultural perspectives including one group who wanted to have smaller bottoms and another group who wanted larger ones. The contrasts were startling in that each wanted the opposite of the other. Much of this appeared to stem from the desire to be sexually attractive. A vox pops street interview with a variety of men indicated that there was no "one size fits all" as a whole variety of opinions were expressed as to what the men saw as being attractive in the opposite sex.

This disturbing trend causes me to question the whole concept of cultural and media stereotypes and the advertising techniques used in the media which create dissatisfaction with our given bodies. The techniques, often using airbrushed celebrities, encourage us to purchase clothes, cosmetics and procedures which purport to make us more like the desired image. It would appear that this is idolatry by media persuasion. We need to become something or someone other than what we are in order to be successful in the perceived culture of the day. This is far from the splendour of the "flowers of the field" that Jesus encouraged. Body acceptance through non-sexual naked interaction would appear to be a prophetic condemnation of our consumerist society.

Cherry Healey on her own blog comments on the encounter which caused her to reassess her whole situation and it necessitates a comprehensive quotation.

"There is light at the end of the tunnel

At the beginning of this process, I suppose, I secretly felt that body liberation couldn't truly exist in a culture with such intensive exposure to images of airbrushed women. But much to my surprise Sandra, a naturist from Gloucester, proved me wrong. Ok, ok, so I know that being a naturist isn't exactly a standard hobby but once I'd acclimatised to seeing people in their birthday suits, I realised that Sandra had a nugget of gold to share. She had taken personal responsibility for her body worries and had decided to change the way she felt about her body. It wasn't a lightening, overnight moment but it was a gradual, conscious decision to feel happier with her body. She chose to see her body in a new light: as an amazing vehicle that had produced six children and was hers and hers alone. She had stopped comparing herself to other women and, in doing so, she had found a happier, more peaceful relationship with her body. I want me some of that." (Cherry Healey)

The above is obviously a single personal opinion but it resonates with many other women whom I have heard commenting in a similar vein. As Naturist Christians, our view of the body as something which gloriously reflects the image of God, is gospel indeed to a society that has been brainwashed into dissatisfaction with our created selves. The simple visual expression of nakedness can bring a deep healing to those oppressed by such media and societal manipulation.

However, we must not lose sight of the need for an inner beauty which is part of the whole person, as God declared to Samuel when he was selecting one of Jesse's sons to be the anointed king, "Do not consider his appearance or his height, for I have rejected him. The LORD does not look at the things human beings look at. People look at the outward appearance, but the LORD looks at the heart." (1 Samuel 16:7)

British Naturism as an organisation does undertake research from time to time to assess the mood of the nation. It has a volunteer Research and Liaison Officer, Malcolm Bourra, who undertakes a considerable amount of work for the organisation particularly as it concerns the public's attitude towards naturism. I have included two appendices at the end of this book which have been produced by him. The latter stems from an opinion poll conducted in 2001 which attempted to research the attitudes which were prevalent in the population at the time. I have recently contacted Malcolm and been given the latest results of a similar poll conducted in September 2011 whose preliminary findings I have included in Appendix 2 *(in italics)* which enable a comparison. The extrapolation of those results would lead to an estimated 3.7 million Naturists in the UK population which is a very significant proportion of society. His initial response to the new figures was that "Society is becoming more polarised. There are many more naturists but a lot fewer people are happy for Naturism to be practised in public places. Both of those changes were expected but we did not expect them to be so large. Unfortunately, despite Naturism becoming a lot more popular, and despite considerable progress on the legal front, the prudification of society is becoming a serious problem."

Attitudes do appear to be changing. Amongst certain areas of society there is perhaps a backlash to the perceived sexualisation of young people and nudity is I believe mistakenly included by some as part of this trend. The Bailey review "Letting Children be Children" published in June 2011 is a direct response to these claims as part of a review commissioned by the UK Government. Whilst I would wholeheartedly approve of many of the recommendations in the review I suspect that the issues raised may well have a detrimental effect with regard to more open attitudes to nudity in general. The review quotes research by Livingston et al. on "Risks and safety for children on the internet" which includes the statement "8 per cent of 11 – 16 year olds report that they have seen online sexual images including nudity. Greater than 6 per cent have seen someone's genitals online." The implication is again that nudity = sex and that the mere observation of genitalia will somehow corrupt the children. It can surely be argued, and indeed is in naturist circles, that the very opposite is true and that hiding the human body creates unhealthy attitudes to sexuality in general. I will return to that subject later.

Another aspect which surely has had a huge impact in this area is the highly publicised cases of sexual abuse particularly in relation to the Roman Catholic Church but found in other churches as well. These cases have a deep impact upon society in general and increase anxiety levels amongst parents and all who have a duty of care for children. Child Protection is high profile throughout Church and society with Criminal Records Bureau checks pervading statutory and voluntary bodies and the private sector as well. This heightened awareness of sexual predation, particularly in regard to vulnerable children and adults, cannot fail to have a knock on effect with regard to anything that might be equated with sex, including the perceived links with nudity. Naturists are only too aware of these issues and take them very seriously with clubs adhering to child protection policies, photographic and video regulations, and the vetting of new members as far as may reasonably be achieved.

Whilst nudity is more commonplace, particularly through the media, there is a backlash as we have seen. Many churches and individuals react to the sexualised view of nudity which permeates our culture by condemning any expression of the nude form. This is surely the proverbial "throwing out the baby with the bath water" scenario. Is it not the case that as Christians we are called upon to redeem the situation, to reclaim the body and put it in its rightful place? The difficulty is that far too often we take our lead from a perceived biblical culture that owes more to a reaction against society than the redeeming of the same through a solid theological critique.

CHAPTER 8

Naked by Nature

Job could declare, ""Naked I came from my mother's womb, and naked I will depart. The LORD gave and the LORD has taken away; may the name of the LORD be praised." (Job 1:21) The same theme is re-iterated by the writer of Ecclesiastes (5:15) and is a continuation of the creation theme in Genesis. The intrinsic value we place upon our bodies, when we recognise that they are a gift from God, encourages us to take good care of them. Looking back through history we can see how clothing developed through the ages, chiefly as a response to the environment in which individuals lived.

A considerable amount of work has been done recently, particularly under the auspices of "The Vitamin D Council" a non-profit organisation looking into the effects of Vitamin D deficiency. Vitamin D is produced naturally by our skin when it comes into contact with sunlight. Keeping our bodies out of the sun and putting on sunblock, alongside an increasing tendency to stay indoors and out of the sun, has meant that there is a major epidemic of Vitamin D deficiency particularly in N. America and Europe. (see Robert P. Heaney)

Clothing enabled people to live under harsher environmental conditions and populate areas of the planet which are otherwise inhospitable. There are complex arguments surrounding skin colour, determined by the level of melanin pigment in the skin and exposure to sunlight. Simply put they state that fair skinned individuals in the more polar latitudes are less protected from the effects of sunlight and so are better able to create Vitamin D whilst those in the equatorial regions have greater pigmentation to protect them from solar damage and have less need for UV absorption for Vitamin D production as they are exposed to stronger sunlight.

A recent article by Bob Berman in the Orlando Sentinel (July 21, 2011) promoting his book "The Sun's Heartbeat: And Other Stories from the Life of the Star That Powers Our Planet" goes so far as to suggest that many maladies of the Western world are as a result of our decreased interaction with the sun. He admits that malignant melanomas are caused by overexposure to UV rays from the sun but argues that the lack of sunlight our bodies are exposed to contributes to the spread of many other cancers and diseases. He describes "an explosion of childhood cases of autism, asthma, and autoimmune disease. It all began when we took our children out of the sun".

An article in the Journal of Virology entitled "On the epidemiology of influenza" in 2008 postulated that vitamin D deficiency may well be linked to the seasonal onset and virulence of flu (Cannell et al.)

Another article in the Journal of Nutrition Research on the "Prevalence and correlates of vitamin D deficiency in US adults" suggested that vitamin D deficiency could be linked to several chronic diseases, including cardiovascular disease and cancer. (Kimberley et al.)

These, and other studies, point to the beneficial effects of sunlight on the exposed skin of the human body. This could be used as part of an argument by design; that this was the way that God created us, and we thrive when we live according to his design parameters. The skin is the largest organ in the human body and is essential for protection against external pathogens and the environment. It acts as a waterproof barrier and provides external sensation, heat regulation, and even nutrient storage. It is immensely complex and is highly efficient, but in order to fulfil its functions effectively it needs to be exposed to the air. My argument from design is that we are designed to function naked. Through our use of clothing we have been enabled to "fill the earth and subdue it" (Genesis 1:28), but the changes of lifestyle and behaviour in recent times through avoidance of sunlight have had dire consequences on our health.

It would be valuable if some robust research into the health of Naturists could be undertaken to corroborate or deny these claims. I am presently unaware of any such research.

Whilst examining issues of health and well-being it would be appropriate to look at the psychological and sociological issues surrounding children and naturism. One of the key arguments promulgated by opponents of naturism is that it will somehow harm the children. By nature children are predisposed to naturism and previous arguments have pointed to the fact that it is our nurture of children which can alienate them from a healthy understanding of the body. Parents of babies will commonly allow some fresh air to surround their babies' bottoms to combat the effects of nappy rash.

Children are only alarmed by nudity if their parents are alarmed. The psychological pressure from parental attitudes is deemed to cause harm in itself through passing on a fear of the human body with all the related consequences of such a fear. Some research has been done in these areas. A study by Marilyn D. Story found that children from nudist family backgrounds had significantly more positive body attitudes than non-nudist family children.

The difficulty with much of the research that has been done is that it is difficult, when dealing with attitudes, to come to definitive conclusions. For instance there is some research, which is oft quoted in Naturist circles, undertaken in 1985 which looked at the different pregnancy and abortion rates between teenagers in the USA and other countries. (Elise F. Jones)

Naturists take such research and come to the conclusion that countries with more tolerant attitudes to nudity on beaches and society in general appear to have significantly less teenage birth rates. However, there are a multitude of competing factors which underlie these figures. It may well be that ignorance about sexuality and the human body are a factor but we cannot draw such hard and fast conclusions from such research simply to further our own position.

There is a widely available document on the internet, reproduced on many naturist sites, which is entitled "205 Arguments and Observations In Support of Naturism - Extensively documented with quotes, references, supporting research, and resources for further study, compiled by K. Bacher." This has all the appearance of a major research paper and does indeed have a very extensive bibliography and list of footnotes. It is an extremely well argued case from a host of different disciplines, which will certainly cause one to consider deeply the issues raised.

Whilst being a valuable document in the armoury of any campaigning naturist it has considerable limitations, chiefly in the availability of the supporting literature. Much is taken from articles in Naturist publications and most attempts to trace the sources can be immensely frustrating. The content itself seems both logical and persuasive, and to someone like myself is highly plausible. I do accept much of what the paper contains but I have to admit that such an exhaustive piece, of what is in effect Naturist propaganda, would benefit from more concrete mainline research support. The difficulty is that, in what is a secretive and often persecuted minority community, little has been done in mainstream research.

Personal experience and conversations with other Naturists may well cause me to support the main tenets of the arguments referred to in the above paper. When one has been persuaded that Naturism is indeed beneficial in so many ways, has the support of scripture and tradition, and has led to a transformation of my own way of life, it takes upon itself the form of an integrated belief system.

One could argue that I am a convert on the crest of a wave, excited by new discoveries and understanding, eager to share my beliefs with others. There are indeed many similarities with my conversion to Christ many years ago. Like many whose lives are transformed into something which is completely opposite to their former selves I have become full of evangelistic fervour. But the Naturist cause is always secondary and subservient to my Christianity. It is certainly complementary, and I believe it enhances my faith and discipleship: but it can never replace it, and obedience to the call of Christ upon my life may even necessitate abstinence. If Isaiah could be called to live naked for three years so too could Bob be called to live clothed. It is not beyond the bounds of faith to believe that God could call upon me to make such a sacrifice and it would be a huge personal sacrifice to undertake.

This has been a long journey of discovery and revelation through which I have undergone a complete transformation of attitude and understanding. Like most journeys it has not always been easy, especially when one looks back at past mistakes and experiences. At the same time discovery and revelation speak of new treasures unearthed, a deeper understanding and appreciation of God's revelation of himself in Jesus, and the "wow" factor of uncovering his image in my own body.

Incarnation is a theological term, pregnant with meaning, which has come full term. The belief that the glory of God became flesh in Jesus, and is revealed in me, has taken on a whole new depth of meaning. There are many lessons in life which we would have preferred to have learnt much earlier. I am saddened that my children never had the opportunity to be raised in a Naturist household and yet I believe God does things in his own good time. Despite my own nurture I have finally discovered my true nature. The image has indeed been uncovered. Thanks be to God.

Appendix 1

Naturist Beliefs

(put together by Malcolm Bourra – Research and Liaison Officer of British Naturism p.5 BN 183)

"Naturists believe that nudity is an enjoyable, natural and moral state which brings benefits to themselves, and to society at large.

Decency and shame

The human body in all its diversity is an object of intrinsic beauty of which the owner should be proud.

Simple nudity is not indecent, shameful, or immoral.

Children

Bringing up children to respect their own and others' bodies, improves their well-being and fosters more responsible sexual behaviour as they grow up.

Children have a right to know what humans really look like.

Social division and respect

Naturism engenders self-respect and respect for others regardless of shape, age, gender, size, colour, or disability.

People should be accepted for who they are and not for what they wear.

Communal nudity discourages social barriers but clothing accentuates social differences.

Clothing

Clothing can provide needed protection but often it is unnecessary and it can be harmful.

Naturism transcends fashion.

In a tolerant society what to wear is a matter of personal choice.

Governments should promote toleration and not impose unnecessary restrictions on freedom.

Environment, nature, and quality of life

Naturism encourages respect for, and harmony with, the environment.

Naturism can add to the quality of life through the enjoyment of simplicity.

Naturism can reduce impact on the environment.

Appendix 2

Statistics - A British Naturism Briefing Paper - Malcolm Boura, Research and Liaison Officer of British Naturism - Updated May 2007 (with additional comparison figures added in 2011)

It is extremely difficult to determine how many naturists there are without a high quality survey. When naturists get dressed the disguise is perfect and naturists do sometimes encounter appalling prejudice so most are very careful whom they let know. Naturism is much more popular and much more generally acceptable than many people believe.

At least 1.2 million people describe themselves as being a naturist which is roughly the same as the membership of the Church of England but it could be double that number.

About 1 person in 4 has swum nude and nearly as many have sunbathed nude. One in five has seen a neighbour nude and a similar number have themselves been nude in their garden. Two thirds said that garden nudity should be legal.

Naturists are considered sensible by nearly half of the general public and a massive 9 out of 10 said that they are harmless. Conversely only 7% thought that naturists were disgusting, a tiny 2% thought that they were criminal and only half of those, 1%, thought that it was criminal enough to be worth informing the police.

Children in the household had no discernible effect on people's attitudes with respect to beach naturism but it did make a small difference for public swimming pools 57/64% and back gardens 64/69%. It is clear that the concerns of some people about families and children are unfounded.

None of the polls and surveys have been repeated so some caution is needed when identifying trends but nudity and naturism do seem to be becoming more common and more accepted.

NOP Poll

A 2001 poll by one of the major polling organisations. Sample size 1823 and demographically representative so it is accurate. *(Alongside this are the preliminary results of a comparative survey conducted during $23^{rd} - 29^{th}$ September 2011 via Capibus, Ipsos-MORI's weekly face-to-face in-home interviews, using computer laptops. Ipsos MORI uses a form of random location sampling and 159 different sampling points were used. The sample comprised of 2,033 respondents aged 15 or over.)*

Experience of unclothed activities 2001 *(2011)*

Have you ever:

a) sunbathed without a costume to get an all-over tan?

14 % *10 %*

b) swum without a costume? 24 % *22 %*

c) been on a foreign naturist beach? 11 % *12 %*

d) visited a British clothes optional beach, resort or Club?

7 % *10 %*

Attitudes to encountering nudity

If you were walking along the coast on a hot day, and you came across a group of naked people sunbathing, swimming or playing cricket, would you:

a) ignore them and keep walking? 78 %

b) be alarmed and keep well away from them? 2 % *5 %*

c) go naked yourself? 2 % *1 %*

d) settle down but keep your swimming costume on?

13 %

e) call the police because you were frightened or distressed?

1

% 1 %

Attitudes to naturists

Naturists enjoy activities such as sunbathing and swimming without clothes. Do you think such people are:

a) criminal? 2 %
1%

b) disgusting? 7 % *9 %*

c) harmless? 88 % *82 %*

d) sensible? 40 % *5 %*

Attitudes to public nudity and the law

If it is not intended to give offence, do you think adult nudity should be legal:

a) in back gardens? 66 % *38 %*

b) in quiet areas of public parks? 10 % *5 %*

d) at certain times in public swimming pools?   35 %   *10 %*

e) anywhere that is specifically declared a "clothing optional" zone?   69 %   *42 %*

and would you describe yourself as a naturist of not?

Yes   2 %   *6 %*

Refused   1 %

No   97 %

Don't know   1 %

Property Finder Poll

A 2006 online poll. A useful addition to our knowledge of public behaviour and attitudes.

84% would buy a home next door to naturists:

• No concerns at all   50%

• Ok if not seen   34%

• Not want to buy   16%

Many people are relaxed about nudity

• Been nude outside at home: 20%

• Seen a neighbour nude: 21%

Younger people are more likely to be free from concerns:

Under 45   59%,

over 45   41%

16% would not want naturists next door but people hate:

Night time party noise   46%

Music through walls or floors   45%

Domestic arguments   39%

Music in garden or balcony   37%

Local authority

Beach visitors, Wirral. Invited to state their dislikes.

Dogs   27.1%,

Litter   14.5%,

Naturist beach 6.8%

Car park   6.3%.

Note close agreement with NOP "disgusting" figure.

Other polls: There have been numerous other, although less reliable polls. The agreement between them is really quite remarkable.

Beach use: In 2001 the National Trust told us that on a good day the naturist beach at Studland has about 2½ thousand users.

Bibliography

References

"BBC - BBC Three Programmes - Cherry's Body Dilemmas." *BBC - Homepage*. N.p., n.d. Web. 27 Sept. 2011. <http://www.bbc.co.uk/programmes/b013y2b1>.

Bacher, K. "205 Arguments and Observations In Support of Naturism | EcoNudes.org " *EcoNudes.org | Reduce the effects of global warming and climate change by taking it off and letting it go!*. N.p., n.d. Web. 28 Sept. 2011. <http://econudes.org/node/28>.

Bailey, Reg. "Figure 5." *Letting Children be Children - Report of an Independent Review of the Commercialisation and Sexualisation of Childhood*. London: Her Majesty's Stationery Office, 2011. 37. Print.

The Naked Office. Barber, Max. Virgin 1. 2009. Television.

Barker, Kenneth L., John H. Stek, and Ronald F. Youngblood. *Zondervan TNIV study Bible: Today's New International Version*. Grand Rapids, Michigan: Zondervan, 2006. Print.

"Barriers to Immersion (Chatzitzot) - Nishmat - Women's Health and Halacha." *Nishmat - The Jeanie Schottenstein Center for Advanced Torah Study for Women*. N.p., n.d. Web. 8 Nov. 2011. <http://www.yoatzot.org/topic.php?id=27>.

Berman, Bob. "Tanning Can Cause Cancer, but Not Tanning Could Cause a Lot Worse." *Gizmodo,*. N.p., 21 July 2011. Web. 28 Sept. 2011. <http://gizmodo.com/5823058/tanning-can-cause-cancer-but-not-tanning-could-cause-a-lot-worse>.

Calendar Girls. Dir. Nigel Cole. Perf. MIRREN Helen, WALTERS Julie, ALDERTON John, BASSETT Linda, CROSBIE Annette. Buena Vista International Touchstone Picture, 2003. DVD.

Cannell, John J , Michael Zasloff, Cedric F Garland, Robert Scragg, and Edward Giovannucci. "On the epidemiology of influenza." *Virology Journal* 5.29 (2008): -. Print.

"Cherry Healey - Cherry's Blog." *Cherry Healey - Home Page*. N.p., n.d. Web. 27 Sept. 2011. <http://www.cherryhealey.com/index.php?option=com_zoo&task=item&item_id=240&Itemid=29>.

Cunningham, Jim C.. *Nudity & Christianity* Bloomington, IN 47403: Authorhouse, 2006. Print.

Cyprien, St. "ANF05. Fathers of the Third Century: Hippolytus, Cyprian, Caius, Novatian, Appendix | Christian Classics Ethereal Library." *Welcome to the CCEL | Christian Classics Ethereal Library*. N.p., n.d. Web. 27 Sept. 2011. <http://www.ccel.org/ccel/schaff/anf05.iv.v.ii.html?highlight=dress,of,virgins#highlight>. "On the dress of Virgins"• Treatise II

"David's fig leaf, perhaps by D. Brucciani & Co., about 1857 - Victoria and Albert Museum." *V&A Home Page - Victoria and Albert Museum*. N.p., n.d. Web. 27 Sept. 2011. <http://www.vam.ac.uk/content/articles/d/davids-fig-leaf/>.

Davidson, Robert. "Gen. 9:18-29." *Genesis 1-11,*. Cambridge: University Press, 1973. 94. Print.

Driver, S. R.. "Studia Biblica et Ecclesiastica, in 5 volumes Preview - Judaic Digital Library (JDL) ." *Welcome to Publishers Row--Online Book Publishing Services*. Varda Books, n.d. Web. 27 Sept. 2011. <http://www.publishersrow.com/Preview/PreviewPage.asp?shid=1&clpg=1&pid=1&bid=3707&fid=31&pg=1531>. Vol.5, "Baptism and Christian Archaeology"• p.239 ff

Farley, Andrew. "5." *The naked Gospel the truth you may never hear in church*. Grand Rapids, Michigan: Zondervan, 2009. 150ff. Print.

Forrest, Kimberley Y. Z. , and Wendy L. Stuhldreher. "Prevalence and correlates of vitamin D deficiency in US adults." *Journal of Nutrition Research* 31. Issue 1 (2011): 48-54. Print.

Goodson, Aileen. "Nudity in Ancient to Modern Cultures-- Aileen Goodson." *Primitivism.* N.p., n.d. Web. 27 Sept. 2011. <http://www.primitivism.com/nudity.htm>.

Gorham, Karen , and Dave Leal. *Naturism and Christianity: are they compatible?.* Cambridge: Grove Books, 2000. Print.

Greenberg, Steven. "2." *Wrestling with God and men: homosexuality in the Jewish tradition.* Madison: University of Wisconsin Press, 2004. 63. Print.

Heaney, Robert P. . "Vitamin D, Nutritional Deficiency, and the Medical Paradigm." *The Journal of Clinical Endocrinology & Metabolism,* vol. 88 .November 1, no. 11 (2003): 5107-5108. Print.

Cherry's Body Dilemmas. Henderson, Ross. BBC Three. 22 Aug. 2011. Television.

Trinny and Susannah Undress the Nation. Hill, Helen. ITV. 2007. Television.

Hippolytus. "The Apostolic Tradition of Hippolytus tr. Burton Scott Easton 1934. ." *Chronicon.Net.* N.p., n.d. Web. 27 Sept. 2011. <www.chronicon.net/chroniconfiles/ApostolicTraditionofHipp olytus.pdf>.

"Home." *INF-FNI International Naturist Federation - Search for naturist resorts, beaches, clubs, and travel..* N.p., n.d. Web. 27 Sept. 2011. <http://www.inffni.org/>.

Howley, ed. G. C. D. , and F. F. Bruce. *A New Testament Commentary .* London: Pickering and Inglis, 1969. Print.

Jerusalem, St. Cyril of. "NPNF2-07. Cyril of Jerusalem ... - St. Cyril of Jerusalem - Google Books." *Google Books*. N.p., n.d. Web. 27 Sept. 2011. <http://books.google.co.uk/books?id=-3WO1xMpCMUC&pg=PT521&lpg=PT521&dq=See+Dict.+Christ.+Antiq.+%E2%80%9CBaptism,%E2%80%9D+%C2%A7+48:+The+Unclothing+of+the+Catechumens:+Bingh.+Ant.+XI.+xi.+1&source=bl&ots=sjN28mTvpo&sig=9rgLx5N3GP O2oOST1V5Shwj6PzI&hl=en&ei>. Dict. Christ. Antiq. "Baptism,"• Â§ 48: The Unclothing of the Catechumens: Bingh. Ant. XI. xi. 1

Jones , Elise F. . "Teenage Pregnancy in Developed Countries: Determinants and Policy Implications." *Family Planning Perspectives* 17.2 (1985): 53-63. Print.

"Medical Devices as Barriers to Mikveh Immersion." *Nishmat - Jewish Women's Health*. N.p., n.d. Web. 27 Sept. 2011. <http://www.jewishwomenshealth.org/article.php?article=10& search=1>.

Meeks, Wayne A., and Jouette M. Bassler. *The HarperCollins study Bible: New Revised Standard Version, with the Apocryphal/Deuterocanonical books*. New York: HarperCollins, 1993. Print.

"Michelangelo. Sistine Chapel. The Last Judgement.." *MoodBook. Bring art to your desktop!*. N.p., n.d. Web. 27 Sept. 2011. <http://www.moodbook.com/history/renaissance/sistine-chapel-last-judgement.html>.

Morris, Leon. "19:23." *The Gospel according to John*. London: Marshall, Morgan & Scott, 1974. 808. Print. footnote: 53

Neal, Matthew. Squeamish Translating summary Web 7 May 2012. http://thebiblicalnaturist.blogspot.co.uk/2012/01/squeamish-translating-summary.html

Osborne, R.. "Men Without Clothes: Heroic Nakedness and Greek Art." *Gender and History* Volume 9 .Number 3 (1997): 504-528. Print.

Petre, Jonathan. "Manchester Cathedral lands in row over nudism | Mail Online." *Home | Mail Online*. N.p., n.d. Web. 27 Sept. 2011. <http://www.dailymail.co.uk/news/article-1375352/Manchester-Cathedral-lands-row-nudism.html>.

Qureshi, Yakub . "Manchester Cathedral to host tarot card readers and healers at 'new age' festival | Manchester Evening News - menmedia.co.uk." *Manchester News, Sport, Football, Business, TV & Showbiz & more | Manchester Evening News - menmedia.co.uk*. N.p., n.d. Web. 27 Sept. 2011. <http://menmedia.co.uk/manchestereveningnews/news/s/1416 452_manchester-cathedral-to-host-tarot-card-readers-and-healers-at-new-age-festival>.

How to look good naked - Gok Wan. REID, Charlotte. Channel 4 (Maverick TV). 2006. Television.

"Register now for The Spirit of Life - Manchester Cathedral." *Welcome to Manchester Cathedral*. N.p., n.d. Web. 27 Sept. 2011. <http://www.manchestercathedral.org/news/36/register-now-for-the-spirit-of-life>.

Rudofsky, Bernard. "Are clothes modern?." *The unfashionable human body*. New York: Doubleday, 1971. 69. Print.

Satlow, Michael L. "Jewish Constructions of Nakedness" JBL 116/3 (1997) [Journal of Biblical Literature]

Saward, Michael . *And so to bed?*. Tonbridge, Kent, UK: Good Reading Limited ;, 1975. Print.

Story , Marilyn D. . "Factors associated with more positive body self-concepts in preschool children." *The Journal of Social Psychology* 108 (1979): 49-56. Print.

"Tate | Glossary | Avant-garde." *Tate: British and international modern and contemporary art*. N.p., n.d. Web.

27 Sept. 2011. <http://www.tate.org.uk/collections/glossary/definition.jsp?ent ryId=38>.

The Full Monty. Dir. Peter Cattaneo. Perf. CARLYLE Robert, WILKINSON Tom, ADDY Mark, SHARP Lesley, WOOF Emily. 20th Century Fox Film Corporation, 1997. VHS.

Tomlinson, Dave. *The Post Evangelical*. London: Triangle, 1995. Print.

Torrance, T. F.. " Proselyte Baptism." *New Testament Studies*, 1 .doi:10.1017/S0028688500003696 (1954): pp 150-154. Print.

"What not to bare: backlash over toplessness on Trinny and Susannah show | Showbiz." *London News | London Evening Standard - London's newspaper*. N.p., n.d. Web. 27 Sept. 2011. <http://www.thisislondon.co.uk/showbiz/article-23420242-what-not-to-bare-backlash-over-toplessness-on-trinny-and-susannah-show.do>.

"Who told you....?." *Fig Leaf Forum: Fellowship, edification and encouragement for Christian nudists and Christian naturists*. N.p., n.d. Web. 27 Sept. 2011. <http://www.figleafforum.com>.

Wojtyla, Karol. *Love and responsibility*. Rev. ed. New York: Farrar, Straus, Giroux, 1981. Print.

"juchre.org - Babylonian Talmud: Sotah 14." *Judeo-Christian Research* . N.p., n.d. Web. 27 Sept. 2011. <http://juchre.org/talmud/sotah/sotah_14.html>.

MLA formatting by BibMe.org.